tastes of
INDIA

JACKI PASSMORE

WELDON
PUBLISHING
SYDNEY · HONG KONG · CHICAGO · LONDON

A Kevin Weldon Production

Published by Weldon Publishing
a division of Kevin Weldon & Associates Pty Limited
372 Eastern Valley Way, Willoughby, NSW 2068, Australia

First published 1991
Reprinted 1992

© Copyright: Kevin Weldon & Associates Pty Limited 1991
© Copyright design: Kevin Weldon & Associates Pty Limited 1991

Printed in Singapore by Kyodo Printing Co (S'pore) Pte Ltd

National Library of Australia Cataloguing-in-Publication data

Passmore, Jacki.
  Tastes of India.

  Includes index.
  ISBN 1 86302 119 1.

  1. Cookery, India. I. Title. (Series :
  Tastes of Asia).

641.5954

*Cover photograph: Carrot dessert, and cream balls in cream sauce
(recipes pages 46 and 48).*

Frontispiece: Baked fish with creamed tomato sauce (recipe page 8).

*Opposite title page: Prawns in green masala, and prawn and green mango curry
(recipes pages 8 and 10).*

CONTENTS

Spices   4

Appetisers   5

Seafood   8

Chicken   12

Eggs   16

Lamb and Mutton   17

Beef and Pork   25

Vegetables   27

Breads   34

Rice Dishes   38

Accompaniments   42

Dhal and Chickpeas   44

Desserts   46

Glossary   50

Index   51

SPICES

SPICES

With the exception of a few freshly made curry pastes purchased from local markets, few Indian cooks would consider using commercial curry powders or pastes in their cooking. Instead, each household is equipped with a spice grinder, either an electric appliance or the time honoured 'curry stone', a granite grinding stone and pestle. Whole fresh spices are ground just before using for maximum freshness. The most commonly used spice blend is garam masala, *which is used in conjunction with other spices, or is used as a condiment and sprinkled on a cooked dish.* Chat masala *is a tart flavoured spice combination particularly good with vegetable dishes. Recipes for these two spice mixes are given below. They may be made in quantity and keep well in an airtight container.*

GARAM MASALA

60 g (2 oz) black peppercorns
60 g (2 oz) cummin seeds
60 g (2 oz) coriander seeds
25 large black cardamoms, peeled
15 g (½ oz) cloves
15 g (½ oz) ground cinnamon

Blend these to a fairly fine powder and pour into a jar with a tight fitting lid. The spice mixture will be even more fragrant if the peppercorns, cummin and coriander are lightly toasted under the griller before grinding.

CHAT MASALA

30 g (1 oz) cummin seeds
1 tablespoon salt
pinch of asafoetida
3 teaspoons chilli powder
2 tablespoons dried green mango powder *(amchur)*
1 tablespoon crushed dried mint
2 teaspoons dried ginger powder

Lightly toast cummin with salt and asafoetida. Grind all ingredients to a fine powder and pour into a jar with a tight fitting lid.

APPETISERS

FRIED VEGETABLE DUMPLINGS

PAKORA

2 large potatoes
2 medium onions
5 spring onions
1 green chilli
1 medium eggplant, or 185 g (6 oz) spinach or cabbage
2 tomatoes
185 g (6 oz) gram flour *(besan)*
2 tablespoons self-raising flour
2 teaspoons salt
2 teaspoons *garam masala*
3 cm (1¼ inch) piece fresh ginger, minced
oil for deep frying

Peel potato, parboil and cut into very small dice. Finely chop onions, spring onions, chilli, eggplant, spinach or cabbage, and tomatoes. Mix with gram flour, self-raising flour, salt, *garam masala* and ginger. Mix to a smooth batter, adding just enough water to make it dropping consistency. Heat oil for deep frying and drop walnut-sized pieces of the batter into the oil and cook to a deep golden brown.
  Drain well, then serve with mint chutney.

CRISP VEGETABLE SNACKS

SAMOOSA

frozen spring roll wrappers
2 large potatoes, boiled
60 g (2 oz) cauliflower, finely chopped
90 g (3 oz) frozen peas
2 tablespoons finely chopped fresh coriander leaves
2.5 cm (1 inch) piece fresh ginger, minced
1 small onion, minced
3 cloves garlic, minced
1 teaspoon chilli powder
½ teaspoon turmeric powder
2½ teaspoons *garam masala*
salt
black pepper
2 teaspoons lemon juice
oil for deep frying

Thaw wrappers and wrap in a damp cloth until needed. Dice cooked potato finely and put into a basin. Drop chopped cauliflower and peas into a bowl of boiling water and leave aside for 5 minutes. Drain well. Mix cauliflower and peas with potatoes and all remaining ingredients except oil and wrappers.
  Cut spring roll wrappers into 4 cm (1½ inch) strips and fold one end over diagonally to make a triangular-shaped pocket. Fill with a spoonful of the mixture. Fold the whole strip over and over to finish with a triangular-shaped cake. Stick end down with a little water or prepare a starch with cornflour and boiling water and use this to glue the flaps.
  Heat oil and deep fry Samoosa until golden. Drain and serve with coriander or mint chutney.

FRIED MEAT SNACKS
MEAT SAMOOSA

frozen spring roll wrappers
250 g (½ lb) minced beef or mutton
¼ cup water
1 clove garlic, minced
1 small onion, minced
1 cm (½ inch) piece fresh ginger, minced
2 teaspoons *garam masala*
1 teaspoon chilli powder
1 teaspoon black mustard seeds
½ teaspoon turmeric powder
salt
black pepper
1 heaped tablespoon chopped fresh coriander leaves
2 tablespoons frozen peas (optional)
2 teaspoons lemon juice
2 tablespoons *ghee*
oil for deep frying

Thaw wrappers and wrap in a damp cloth until needed. Cook minced meat in water until the liquid has completely dried up. Fry minced garlic and onion in *ghee* for 3 minutes. Add ginger, meat and *garam masala* and fry for a further 3 minutes. Add remaining ingredients and heat through thoroughly. Leave to cool.

Cut spring roll wrappers into 4 cm (1½ inch) strips and fold one end over diagonally to make a triangular-shaped pocket. Fill with the mixture and continue folding in this triangular shape until all folded. Stick the end down with a little water or prepare a starch with cornflour and boiling water and use to glue the flaps.

Heat oil and deep fry Samoosa until golden. Drain and serve hot with mint chutney.

SCRAMBLED EGGS PARSI STYLE
AKURI

6 large eggs
salt
black pepper
pinch of turmeric powder
3 tablespoons *ghee*
1 large onion
1 green chilli
3 tablespoons fresh coriander leaves
1 fresh red chilli, thinly sliced

Beat eggs lightly with salt, pepper and turmeric powder. Mince or finely chop onion, chilli and coriander. Heat *ghee* in a frying pan and add chopped ingredients to the pan. Fry for 3 minutes on moderate heat, then reduce heat slightly and pour in beaten egg.

Cook, stirring frequently, until egg is just set. Check seasoning. Garnish with thinly sliced chilli and serve with fresh buttered toast.

COLD LENTIL CAKES IN YOGHURT SAUCE

250 g (½ lb) yellow lentils, soaked overnight
1 medium onion
2 teaspoons salt
2 teaspoons *garam masala*
½ teaspoon chilli powder
2 teaspoons baking powder
pinch of asafoetida (optional)
ghee or oil for deep frying
2½ cups plain yoghurt
1 tablespoon thick cream (optional)
salt
pepper
sugar
2 teaspoons finely chopped mint

Rinse lentils and drain well. Put into a heavy duty grinder and grind to a smooth paste. It may be necessary to add a little water to prevent machine clogging. Mince onion and add to the lentil paste with salt, *garam masala*, chilli powder, baking powder and asafoetida (if used). Mix thoroughly, then form the paste into walnut sized balls using wet or greased hands. If needed add a little plain flour or gram flour *(besan)* to bind.

Heat oil and drop in several balls at a time. Deep fry to a light golden brown. Lift out and drain thoroughly. Fry a second time for about 2 minutes on moderate heat and drain well.

Whip yoghurt with cream (if used) and season with salt, pepper and sugar to taste. Place lentil cakes in a serving dish and pour on the yoghurt sauce. Garnish with chopped mint. Chill slightly, leaving for at least 1 hour before serving to allow lentil cakes to soften.

MULLIGATAWNY SOUP

250 g (½ lb) chicken
5 cups chicken stock
1 large onion
3 cloves garlic
2 fresh red chillies, thinly sliced
2 tablespoons *ghee*
1 tablespoon coriander, ground
¼ teaspoon fenugreek, crushed
1 teaspoon cummin, ground
1 teaspoon turmeric powder
1 bay leaf
2.5 cm (1 inch) stick cinnamon
2 black cardamoms
2 cloves
salt
pepper
¾ cup thick coconut milk

Place chicken and stock in a large saucepan with sliced onion. Bring to the boil and simmer for 30 minutes. Mash garlic and chillies and fry in *ghee* for 2 minutes. Add all remaining spices and fry for 2 minutes. Add to the pot and continue cooking until chicken is tender.

Lift out chicken and cut into small dice. Return to the soup. Season to taste and stir in thick coconut milk. Heat through.

SEAFOOD

PRAWNS IN GREEN MASALA

750 g (1½ lb) raw prawns, in shells
2 medium onions
2 cloves garlic
2.5 cm (1 inch) piece fresh ginger
1 teaspoon fennel
½ teaspoon cummin
2 green chillies
5 tablespoons chopped fresh coriander leaves
1 teaspoon salt
2 tablespoons *ghee* or coconut oil
¾ cup water

Peel prawns, leaving heads and tails on. Slice one onion thinly and make a seasoning paste by grinding remaining onion with all other ingredients except *ghee* or oil.

Fry sliced onion in *ghee* or oil until soft, then add seasoning paste and fry for 4 minutes. Add water and simmer until sauce is thick and smooth. Put in prawns and cook for about 5 minutes, or until tender. Do not overcook. Check seasonings and serve at once.

Thinly sliced fish fillets may also be cooked in this sauce.

BAKED FISH WITH CREAMED TOMATO SAUCE

750 g (1½ lb) snapper, bream or other meaty fish
3 tablespoons *ghee*
1¼ teaspoons fenugreek, ground
4 cloves garlic, crushed
2.5 cm (1 inch) piece fresh ginger, minced
1 tablespoon coriander, ground
2 teaspoons cummin, ground
1½ teaspoons chilli powder
¾ teaspoon turmeric powder
6 medium tomatoes, peeled
¾ cup water or fish stock
½ cup thick cream
¼ cup plain yoghurt
salt
black pepper
lemon juice

Clean fish, remove scales and clip fins. Wipe dry.

Heat *ghee* in a small saucepan. Fry fenugreek, garlic and ginger in the *ghee* for 3 minutes, then add coriander, cummin, chilli and turmeric. Fry for 2 minutes, stirring frequently.

Chop tomatoes finely and add to the pan with water or stock. Cover and simmer until sauce is thick and creamy. Add cream and yoghurt and season to taste with salt and black pepper. Keep warm.

Sprinkle fish with salt, pepper and lemon juice and place in a lightly oiled oven-proof dish. Cover with a piece of foil and bake in a moderately hot oven for 15 minutes. Remove foil and cook for a further 5 minutes. Remove from the oven. Pour on hot sauce and return to the oven for 5 minutes before serving.

FISH KEBABS

500 g (1 lb) meaty white fish
1 cm (½ inch) piece fresh ginger, minced
2 tablespoons boiling water
¾ cup plain yoghurt
1 teaspoon fennel seeds, crushed
1 teaspoon cummin, ground
¼ teaspoon black pepper
1½ teaspoons chilli powder
pinch of ground cloves
2 curry leaves (optional)
1 teaspoon salt
1 large onion
1 green pepper
2 limes
lime or lemon juice
dry green mango powder *(amchur)*
ghee

Cut fish into 2 cm (¾ inch) cubes. Pour boiling water over ginger and leave for 10 minutes, then strain liquid over fish. Leave for 20 minutes. Mix yoghurt with fennel, cummin, pepper, chilli powder, clove powder, crumbled curry leaves (if used) and salt and rub into the fish pieces. Marinate for 2 hours.

Cut onion into thin slices and pull into rings. Cut pepper into thin circles. Cut lemons into wedges and place with onion and pepper on a serving plate. Thread fish onto skewers and brush with a little melted *ghee*. Roast over a charcoal fire or under the griller until cooked through but do not overcook. Sprinkle with dried mango powder and place on the plate with onion, pepper and limes. Serve hot.

GOAN CURRIED FISH

750 g (1½ lb) white fish fillets
1 tablespoon lemon juice
5 dried chillies, soaked
1 teaspoon cummin seeds
3 teaspoons coriander seeds
60 g (2 oz) grated fresh or desiccated coconut
6 cloves garlic
1 small onion
2 medium onions
3 cm (1¼ inch) piece fresh ginger
4 tablespoons *ghee* or 3 tablespoons coconut oil
¾ teaspoon turmeric powder
2 green chillies, thinly sliced
1 tablespoon finely chopped fresh coriander leaves
1½ tablespoons tamarind
1½ cups water
salt
sugar to taste

Cut fish into 5 cm (2 inch) pieces and sprinkle with lemon juice.

Grind ingredients from chillies to small onion to a paste. Thinly slice medium onions and shred ginger. Fry in *ghee* or oil for 4 minutes, then put in spicy coconut paste and fry for 2 minutes. Add turmeric, sliced chillies and chopped coriander. Infuse tamarind in water, strain and add to pan. Bring to the boil, reduce heat and simmer for 15 minutes.

Add sliced fish and cook gently for about 6 minutes. Season to taste with salt and sugar. Serve at once.

FISH IN COCONUT SAUCE

625 g (1 ¼ lb) thin fillets of white fish
2 large onions
2 green chillies
2.5 cm (1 inch) piece fresh ginger
4 cm (1½ inch) stalk lemon grass
3 cloves garlic
2 teaspoons dried shrimps, soaked
45 g (1½ oz) desiccated coconut
1 cup thick coconut milk
2 tablespoons coconut oil or vegetable oil
2 heaped tablespoons finely chopped fresh coriander
    leaves
1 cup thin coconut milk
lemon juice or tamarind water
salt

Cut fish fillets into 5 cm (2 inch) squares and place in a
dish. Thinly slice one onion and set aside. Mince ginger, lemon grass, garlic, dried shrimps and desiccated
coconut to a fairly smooth paste and add thick coconut
milk. Pour over the fish and marinate for 1 hour.
    Heat oil and fry sliced onion until lightly coloured.
Add fish pieces and cook briefly, then pour on thin
coconut with coriander and marinade. Cover and simmer on low heat until fish is cooked. Lift out fish with a
slotted spoon and place on a serving dish.
    Continue to simmer sauce until thick and creamy.
Season to taste with lemon juice or tamarind water and
add salt. Pour over the fish and serve at once.

PRAWN AND GREEN MANGO CURRY

375 g (¾ lb) raw peeled prawns
2 large green mangoes
45 g (1½ oz) freshly grated or desiccated coconut
3 teaspoons coriander, ground
½ teaspoon chilli powder
6 dried chillies, soaked
2 tablespoons water
2 medium onions
3 tablespoons *ghee,* or 2 tablespoons coconut oil
2 curry leaves
2 cups water
¾ teaspoon turmeric powder
salt
fresh coriander leaves
⅓ cup thick coconut milk (optional)

Rinse prawns and remove dark veins, if any. Peel and
slice mangoes. Grind coconut, coriander, chilli powder
and chillies to a paste, adding water.
    Thinly slice onions. Fry onions in *ghee* or coconut oil
for 2 minutes, then add curry leaves and the coconut
paste. Continue to fry until oil begins to rise to the surface. Add the prawns and mango, water, turmeric and
salt and simmer on moderately low heat until cooked.
    Garnish with fresh coriander leaves. For a thicker
curry, stir in coconut milk and heat through.

MASALA STUFFED FISH

1 whole flat fish weighing 625 g (1¼ lb) (John Dory,
    pomfret or turbot)
3 green chillies
60 g (2 oz) desiccated coconut
1 cm (½ inch) piece fresh ginger
3 cloves garlic
2 teaspoons lemon juice
¼ teaspoon fennel seeds, lightly crushed
1 teaspoon salt
pinch of white pepper
½ teaspoon chilli powder
1 tablespoon chopped fresh coriander leaves
6 shallots
oil for shallow frying
tomato and lemon wedges
onion slices or rings

Clean fish and trim fins. Carefully cut away backbone
working through the stomach opening.

Grind all seasoning ingredients including coriander
leaves and shallots to a paste and stuff into the fish. Sew
up carefully or secure opening with toothpicks.

Heat oil and fry fish on both sides to a golden brown.
Turn once only. Lift onto a serving plate and garnish
with tomato and lemon wedges and onion.

CRAB KORMA

4 medium raw crabs
30 g (1 oz) desiccated coconut
2 teaspoons cummin
1½ tablespoons coriander
1 teaspoon fennel
pinch of powdered cinnamon
1 teaspoon turmeric
1 tablespoon white poppy seeds
3 cloves garlic
5 dried chillies, soaked
1 cm (½ inch) piece fresh ginger
1 small onion
¾ cup plain yoghurt
2 tablespoons *ghee* or coconut oil
4 cloves
1 teaspoon black peppercorns, lightly crushed
4 black cardamoms, lightly crushed
2.5 cm (1 inch) stick cinnamon
1¼ cups water
salt
lemon juice
chopped fresh coriander leaves

Wash crabs and chop into large pieces. Crack claws.
Grind desiccated coconut, cummin, coriander, fennel,
cinnamon, turmeric and poppy seeds to a powder.
Grind garlic, chillies, ginger and onion to a paste. Mix
spice powder and onion paste with yoghurt.

Heat *ghee* and fry cloves, peppercorns, cardamoms
and cinnamon stick for 1 minute. Add crabs and cook,
turning frequently, for 2 minutes. Add seasoning paste
and cook, stirring, until the seasonings are dried up and
clinging to the crab. Pour in water and simmer until
crabs are cooked.

Lift out crab and place on a serving dish. Continue to
simmer sauce until well reduced. Season to taste with
salt and lemon juice and stir in coriander leaves. Pour
over the crab and serve.

CHICKEN

CHICKEN KASHMIR

DUM MURGHI KASHMIR

This chicken is cooked in two stages: marinated and roasted, then rubbed with a spice paste and fried.

1.5 kg (3 lb) chicken
6 cloves garlic
2.5 cm (1 inch) piece fresh ginger
1 green chilli
1 tablespoon lemon juice
1 teaspoon *garam masala*
1 teaspoon chilli powder
½ teaspoon salt
¼ teaspoon turmeric powder
½ cup plain yoghurt
½ teaspoon sugar

Clean the chicken and wipe dry. Grind all ingredients except yoghurt and sugar to a paste, then stir in yoghurt and sugar. Rub over the chicken, inside and out. Leave for 2 hours to absorb the flavours. Roast in a moderate oven until almost cooked through, then remove from oven and leave to cool completely.

Curry paste:
1 large onion
4 cloves garlic
2.5 cm (1 inch) piece fresh ginger
6 cloves
1 teaspoon black peppercorns
2.5 cm (1 inch) stick cinnamon
1 heaped teaspoon fennel seeds
2 tablespoons coriander
6 black cardamoms
1 teaspoon cummin
45 g (1½ oz) ground almonds
1 teaspoon salt
¼ cup plain yoghurt
¼ teaspoon saffron powder
2 tablespoons boiling water
1 teaspoon *garam masala*
1 tablespoon finely chopped fresh coriander leaves
4 tablespoons *ghee*

Mince onion with garlic and ginger. Grind all spices to a fine powder and mix with onion paste. Add almonds, salt, yoghurt and saffron steeped in boiling water. Rub this mixture over the chicken.

Add *ghee* to the pan and cook chicken, basting frequently with *ghee* and the sauce, until chicken is done.

Sprinkle with *garam masala* and chopped coriander leaves before serving.

12

Opposite: Pakoras and samoosas (recipes pages 5–6).
Overleaf: Chicken Kashmir (recipe this page).

TANDOORI CHICKEN

6 chicken thighs
1 small onion, grated
3 cloves garlic, minced
juice of 1 lemon
2 teaspoons salt
3 dried chillies
1 teaspoon turmeric powder
1 teaspoon fenugreek seeds, ground
3 teaspoons coriander
1½ teaspoons cummin
1½ teaspoons black mustard seeds
2 teaspoons chilli powder
½ teaspoon red colouring powder
¾ cup plain yoghurt
softened *ghee*
dried green mango powder *(amchur)*
lemon wedges
onion rings

Prick chicken thighs with a skewer and remove skin.
Rub with a mixture of grated onion, garlic, lemon juice
and salt. Leave for 20 minutes.
   Grind chillies with remaining spices and mix with red
colouring powder and yoghurt. Rub this mixture well
into the chicken, cover and leave overnight.
   Brush with *ghee* and bake in a moderately hot oven
or under a moderate grill until cooked through. Brush
with more *ghee* during cooking.
   Sprinkle with mango powder and serve with lemon
wedges and onion rings.

YOGHURT CHICKEN

1.5 kg (3 lb) chicken
1 teaspoon turmeric
1 tablespoon coriander, ground
1 teaspoon cummin
1½ teaspoons chilli powder
½ teaspoon fenugreek seeds, ground
1 large onion, minced
2 cloves garlic, minced
2.5 cm (1 inch) piece fresh ginger, minced
1½ cups plain yoghurt
4 tablespoons *ghee*
1 large onion
3 cloves garlic
3 black cardamoms, peeled
3 cloves
2.5 cm (1 inch) stick cinnamon
salt
black pepper
lemon juice
fresh coriander leaves or mint, chopped

Wipe chicken and cut into large pieces. Place in a bowl
and rub with turmeric. Make a paste with spices,
onions, garlic and ginger. Mix with the yoghurt, pour
over the chicken and leave to marinate for 2 hours.
Turn several times.
   Heat *ghee* and fry sliced onion and garlic until soft.
Add cardamoms, cloves and cinnamon stick. Add
marinated chicken and cook until well coloured. Add
any remaining marinade and enough water to just cover
the chicken. Cover and simmer until tender. Season to
taste with salt, pepper and lemon juice.
   Garnish with fresh coriander or mint.   **13**

Overleaf: Braised lamb with fruit and nuts (recipe page 18).
Opposite: Kebabs of minced lamb (recipe page 20).

COCONUT CURRIED CHICKEN

1.5 kg (3 lb) chicken
salt
2 medium onions
1 clove garlic
1½ teaspoons chilli powder
2 tablespoons desiccated coconut, ground
1 teaspoon turmeric powder
4 cm (1½ inch) piece fresh ginger, shredded
1 tablespoon dried shrimps, soaked
10 cm (4 inch) stalk lemon grass, quartered
2 tablespoons coconut oil
2 cups thin coconut milk
6 small new potatoes
salt
lemon juice
fresh coriander leaves, finely chopped

Clean and wipe chicken and cut into large pieces. Season with salt. Grind onions and garlic to a paste and add chilli, coconut, turmeric and ginger. Grind dried shrimps and add to the seasoning with lemon grass. Heat oil and fry seasoning paste for 3 minutes, stirring constantly. Add chicken and cook until well coloured.

Pour on coconut milk, cover and simmer until chicken is tender. Peel potatoes, add to the curry and continue cooking until soft and the sauce has thickened. Add salt and lemon juice to taste and garnish with chopped coriander leaves.

CHICKEN IN WHITE CURRY

MURGH MUSSALAM

1.5 kg (3 lb) chicken
salt
black pepper
2 tablespoons *ghee*
1 large onion, minced
4 cloves garlic, crushed
2.5 cm (1 inch) piece fresh ginger, minced
1 tablespoon coriander, ground
3 cloves, crushed
1 teaspoon black peppercorns, crushed
2 teaspoons cummin, ground
2 bay leaves
60 g (2 oz) white poppy seeds, soaked overnight
2 cups water
½ cup thick cream
chilli powder
1 tablespoon finely chopped fresh coriander leaves

Clean chicken and wipe dry. Cut into large pieces and rub with salt and pepper. Melt *ghee* in a heavy pan and fry onion and garlic for 3 minutes on moderate heat. Add ginger and spices and fry for a further 3 minutes. Put in chicken and cook until well coloured. Add bay leaves.

Grind poppy seeds to a smooth paste. Add ½ cup water to the pot and simmer until dried up, then add remaining water and poppy seeds and simmer until the sauce is thick and creamy and chicken tender. Stir in thick cream and add salt, pepper and chilli powder to taste.

Garnish with chopped coriander leaves.

TIKKA CHICKEN

This recipe is a simplified version of Tandoori chicken.

750 g (1½ lb) chicken breasts
1 medium onion
3 cloves garlic
2.5 cm (1 inch) piece fresh ginger
¼ cup plain yoghurt
2 teaspoons white vinegar
2 teaspoons chilli powder
2 teaspoons coriander, ground
1 teaspoon cummin, ground
½ teaspoon turmeric powder
salt
lemon juice
garam masala
onion rings
lemon wedges
lettuce leaves

Cut chicken into 5 cm (2 inch) squares and press flat.
    Grind onion, garlic and ginger to a paste and mix with yoghurt. Add vinegar and spices and rub well into the chicken. Leave for 3 hours to marinate.
    Sprinkle with salt and thread onto skewers. Place under a hot grill or over a charcoal barbecue to cook until tender with crisp surface.
    Sprinkle with lemon juice and *garam masala* and serve on a bed of lettuce leaves surrounded with onion rings and lemon wedges.

CHICKEN CURRY

1 kg (2 lb) chicken pieces
2 large onions
5 cloves garlic
2.5 cm (1 inch) piece fresh ginger
3 tablespoons *ghee*
2 black cardamoms
4 cloves
5 cm (2 inch) stick cinnamon
2 bay leaves
2 blades mace
1 tablespoon coriander, ground
1 teaspoon cummin, ground
¾ teaspoon turmeric powder
½ teaspoon chilli powder
water or light chicken stock
salt
black pepper
1 teaspoon *garam masala*
2 tablespoons finely chopped fresh coriander leaves
lemon juice

Cut chicken pieces into 5 cm (2 inch) cubes. Thinly slice onions and garlic and shred ginger. Heat *ghee* and fry onions until soft. Add garlic and ginger and cook for 1 minute, then put in chicken pieces and fry until well coloured.
    Add all the spices and stir on moderate heat for 5 minutes. Add enough water or light chicken stock to just cover. Bring to the boil and simmer until chicken is very tender and liquid almost evaporated. Add salt and pepper to taste and pour in more water or chicken stock to just cover. Simmer for a further 20 minutes, then sprinkle in *garam masala*, coriander leaves and add lemon juice to taste.

EGGS

CURRIED EGGS

8 large eggs
2 tablespoons *ghee*
5 shallots, thinly sliced
2 cloves garlic, crushed
1 green chilli, chopped
1 cm (½ inch) piece fresh ginger, shredded
2 teaspoons dried prawns, soaked and ground
½ teaspoon fennel seeds
1 teaspoon fenugreek seeds, lightly crushed
1 teaspoon turmeric powder
1½ cups thin coconut milk
½ cup thick coconut milk
lemon juice
salt
pepper
1 tablespoon finely chopped fresh coriander leaves

Place eggs in a pan of cold water and boil for 10 minutes. Run eggs under cold water, peel, cover with cold water and set aside. Heat *ghee* and fry shallots and garlic until soft. Add chilli, ginger, dried prawns, fennel and fenugreek and fry for 4 minutes, stirring frequently. Sprinkle on turmeric and add whole or halved boiled eggs. Turn to coat evenly with the seasonings, and fry for 3 minutes.

Pour on thin coconut milk and simmer for 10 minutes, then add thick coconut milk and season to taste with lemon juice, salt and pepper. Heat through and stir in chopped coriander.

EGG MASALA

6 large eggs
2 green chillies
1 cm (½ inch) piece fresh ginger
60 g (2 oz) desiccated coconut
2 teaspoons cummin
1 tablespoon coriander
1 large onion
2 tablespoons *ghee*
1 teaspoon black mustard seeds
1 teaspoon turmeric powder
2 large tomatoes, chopped
1 cup water
tamarind water or lemon juice
salt
pepper

Place eggs in a pan of cold water and boil for 10 minutes. Cover with cold water and set aside.

Grind chillies and ginger to a paste then grind with coconut, cummin and coriander. Thinly slice onion and fry in *ghee* until soft. Add seasoning paste and fry for 2 minutes. Sprinkle on mustard seeds and turmeric and add tomato and water. Bring to the boil and simmer for 10 minutes. Season to taste with tamarind water or lemon juice, salt and pepper.

Peel eggs and cut in halves, lengthways. Place in the masala and simmer for 3 minutes.

16

LAMB AND MUTTON

LAMB IN SPINACH PUREE

750 g (1½ lb) leg or shoulder of lamb
3 tablespoons *ghee*
3 cloves garlic, crushed
2.5 cm (1 inch) piece fresh ginger, grated
4 black cardamoms, crushed
1 tablespoon coriander, ground
½ green chilli, finely chopped
2 teaspoons black mustard seeds, ground
1 teaspoon turmeric powder
1½ cups water
2 teaspoons salt
750 g (1½ lb) fresh or frozen leaf spinach
pinch of freshly grated nutmeg
1½ teaspoons sugar
1 tablespoon white poppy seeds, ground
¼ cup plain yoghurt
salt
½ cup thick cream

Trim meat and cut into 4 cm (1½ inch) cubes. Heat *ghee* in a casserole or heavy saucepan and fry garlic for 2 minutes. Add ginger, crushed cardamoms, coriander, chilli and mustard seeds and fry on moderate heat for 2 minutes. Add meat and sprinkle on turmeric. Stir to coat meat thoroughly with the spices and cook for 5 minutes.

Pour on ½ cup water, cover pot and cook for 20 minutes. Add remaining water and salt and cook, covered, until lamb is tender and most of the liquid absorbed.

Drain frozen spinach, or wash and drain fresh spinach, discarding stems. Chop finely and put into a saucepan with nutmeg, sugar, poppy seeds and yoghurt. Cover and cook until tender. Add salt to taste and blend to a puree in a liquidiser. Add to the meat and heat through, stirring to mix the two sauces well. Add thick cream and reheat.

Check seasoning and serve hot.

BRAISED LAMB WITH FRUIT AND NUTS

750 g (1½ lb) boned young lamb, leg or shoulder
3 cups water
1 tablespoon lemon juice
2 bay leaves
5 cm (2 inch) stick cinnamon
4 tablespoons *ghee*
5 cm (2 inch) piece fresh ginger, shredded
6 cloves garlic, crushed
2 large onions, minced
6 green cardamoms, crushed
2 tablespoons coriander, ground
3 cloves
1 tablespoon white poppy seeds
45 g (1½ oz) ground almonds
1 teaspoon black pepper
2 tablespoons finely chopped fresh mint
¾ cup plain yoghurt
2 teaspoons *garam masala*
1 teaspoon chilli powder
salt
45 g (1½ oz) raisins, soaked
30 g (1 oz) sultanas, soaked
45 g (1½ oz) blanched, slivered almonds
¼ teaspoon saffron
1 tablespoon boiling water
1½ teaspoons rose water (optional)

Place trimmed lamb in a pot and add water, lemon juice, bay leaves and cinnamon. Cover and bring to the boil, then reduce heat and simmer for about 1 hour until very tender. Skim several times during cooking. Remove meat and reduce liquid to about ¾ cup.

Heat 3 tablespoons *ghee* and fry ginger, garlic and onions until soft. Grind cardamoms, coriander, cloves, poppy seeds, almonds and black pepper to a powder and add to the pan. Fry for 3 minutes, stirring frequently. Add mint and yoghurt and simmer until sauce is thick and creamy.

Add the meat and spoon the sauce over it. Braise until heated through and well seasoned. Add reserved stock and simmer uncovered, until the liquid is completely absorbed or evaporated. Sprinkle on *garam masala*, chilli powder and salt.

Melt remaining *ghee* and fry drained fruit and nuts gently for 5 minutes. Add to the pan. Mix saffron with boiling water and rose water. Pour over the meat and heat through, or cover and place in a moderate oven for 15 minutes.

DHANSAK WITH BROWN RICE

375 g (¾ lb) mixed lentils (black, yellow, red,
  chickpeas, etc)
750 g (1½ lb) lamb shoulder or leg
90 g (3 oz) pumpkin
125 g (¼ lb) spinach
1 large onion
3 tablespoons chopped fresh coriander leaves
2 teaspoons turmeric powder
2 teaspoons salt
4 dried chillies, soaked
2 teaspoons tamarind
3 tablespoons boiling water
2.5 cm (1 inch) piece fresh ginger
6 cloves garlic
2 green chillies
3 cloves
5 cm (2 inch) stick cinnamon
3 green cardamoms
1 teaspoon black mustard seeds
1 tablespoon ground coriander
2 teaspoons ground cummin
3 tablespoons chopped fresh coriander leaves
salt
pepper
1 large onion, finely chopped
3 tablespoons *ghee*

If using hard lentils like black or green lentils or chickpeas, soak overnight, then boil for 3 hours to soften.
Place all lentils, well washed, into a saucepan and add
meat cut into 1 cm (½ inch) dice. Cover with water to 8
cm (3 inches) above the level of the ingredients and
bring to the boil. Simmer for at least 1 hour.
  Peel and slice pumpkin, chop spinach and slice
onion. Add pumpkin, spinach, coriander leaves, onion,
turmeric and salt to the pan and cook until meat and
lentils are tender. Remove meat and place in another
pan. Mash lentils with vegetables or put in a blender to
puree.
  Grind seasonings (from dried chillies to green
chillies) to a paste. Soak tamarind in water and add to
paste together with cloves, cinnamon, cardamom and
mustard seeds. Add ground coriander and cummin.
  Heat *ghee* and fry seasonings for 4 minutes, then add
fresh coriander, salt, pepper and finely chopped onion.
Cook for a further 3 minutes, then put in lamb and
cook until well coloured. Add lentil puree and adjust
seasoning to taste. Heat through.
  Keep warm while rice is prepared.

Brown Rice:
315 g (10 oz) long grain rice
2 large onions
2 tablespoons *ghee*
4 cloves
2 black cardamoms
5 cm (2 inch) stick cinnamon
salt
sugar
pepper

Wash rice and drain well. Chop onions finely and fry in
ghee until very well coloured. They should be very dark
brown, almost black. Add spices and rice and cover
with water to 3 cm (1¼ inch) above the rice. Cover and
bring to the boil. Simmer until cooked through. Season
to taste with salt, pepper and sugar.

KEBABS OF MINCED LAMB

SHEEK KEBAB

750 g (1½ lb) boneless lamb, finely minced
¼ teaspoon saffron powder
2 tablespoons water
2 teaspoons cummin, ground
1 large onion, minced
3 cloves garlic, crushed
2½ tablespoons finely chopped fresh coriander leaves
1½ teaspoons salt
3 tablespoons ghee
dried green mango powder *(amchur)*
lettuce leaves
lime wedges
onion rings

Mix all ingredients except 1 tablespoon *ghee* and dried green mango powder together and knead until smooth. Divide into 5 cm (2 inch) balls and flatten each into a sausage shape. Insert a flat metal skewer along each kebab, press firmly onto the skewer and roll across the bottom of a plate to give an even shape.

Melt remaining *ghee* and brush each kebab lightly. Cook under a hot grill or on a charcoal barbecue until well browned on the surface and cooked through. Brush with more *ghee* during cooking to keep moist. Remove from heat and sprinkle with mango powder.

Serve with lime wedges and onion rings on a bed of lettuce leaves.

LAMB AND POTATO CURRY

500 g (1 lb) lean lamb, shoulder or leg
250 g (½ lb) peeled potatoes
oil for deep frying
2 large onions
2 black cardamoms
¼ teaspoon fennel seeds
1 tablespoon coriander, ground
¾ teaspoon turmeric powder
2.5 cm (1 inch) piece fresh ginger
4 cloves garlic
2 green chillies
½ cup plain yoghurt
3 tablespoons *ghee*
1½ teaspoons black mustard seeds
½ teaspoon chilli powder
salt
black pepper
garam masala
fresh coriander leaves, finely chopped

Trim lamb and cut into 4 cm (1½ inch) cubes. Cut potatoes into 2 cm (¾ inch) dice. Heat oil and fry potatoes until well coloured. Remove and drain well.

Slice onions thinly. Grind seasonings from cardamoms to chillies to a fairly smooth paste and rub into the meat cubes. Place in a dish and pour on yoghurt. Leave for 2 hours to marinate.

Heat *ghee* and fry lamb until well coloured. Add any remaining marinade, sliced onion and cover with water. Bring to the boil, cover and simmer until meat is very tender. Add fried potatoes and mustard seeds and season with chilli powder, salt, pepper and *garam masala* to taste. Heat through, transfer to a serving dish and garnish with chopped coriander leaves.

MINCED MUTTON WITH PEAS

KEEMA MUTTAR

500 g (1 lb) minced mutton
1 large onion
3 cloves garlic
1 cm (½ inch) piece fresh ginger
3 tablespoons *ghee*
1 teaspoon chilli powder
1½ teaspoons *garam masala*
1 teaspoon black mustard seeds
½ teaspoon turmeric powder
3 medium tomatoes
185 g (6 oz) frozen peas
¾ cup water
salt
pepper
1 tablespoon finely chopped fresh coriander leaves

Boil mutton in a little water until cooked through and all liquid dried up. Set aside. Finely mince onion with garlic and ginger. Fry in *ghee* until soft, then add minced meat, chilli powder, *garam masala,* mustard seeds and turmeric. Fry for 3 minutes, stirring constantly.

Peel tomatoes and chop finely; add to the pan with peas. Pour in water and bring to the boil. Cover, reduce heat and simmer for 15 minutes. Season to taste with salt and pepper and stir in coriander leaves.

SAVOURY MINCED MEAT

RESHMI KIMA

250 g (½ lb) boneless mutton
6 cloves garlic
1 small onion
2.5 cm (1 inch) piece fresh ginger
½ cup water
2 tablespoons *ghee*
1 teaspoon salt
1 teaspoon *garam masala*
pinch of chilli powder
pinch of black pepper
1 tablespoon finely chopped fresh coriander leaves

Mince mutton with garlic, onion and ginger. Boil with
water until all liquid has dried up and meat is well
coloured. Add *ghee,* salt, *garam masala,* chilli powder
and black pepper and fry for 5 minutes, stirring frequently. Add coriander and mix in well.
   Serve with Chupati or fresh toast as a snack or break-
fast dish.

MUTTON WITH FRIED OKRA

BHINDI GOSHT

500 g (1 lb) lean mutton, shoulder or leg
2 medium onions
3 tablespoons *ghee*
3 cloves garlic
2.5 cm (1 inch) piece fresh ginger
2 heaped teaspoons *garam masala*
1½ cups water
2 teaspoons salt
375 g (¾ lb) small okra
oil for deep frying

Trim mutton and cut into 2.5 cm (1 inch) cubes. Slice
onions thinly and fry in *ghee* until soft. Mince garlic
and ginger and add to the pan. Fry for 3 minutes, then
put in meat and cook until well coloured. Sprinkle on
garam masala and cook for 3 minutes, then pour on
water and bring to the boil. Reduce heat and simmer
until meat is tender. Season with salt.
   Trim tops of okra and cut each in halves. Heat oil and
deep fry the okra until slightly crisp. Lift out and drain
well. Place in the pan with meat and heat through for 4
minutes.
   Sliced eggplant may be added in place of okra.
Sprinkle with a little salt and leave for 10 minutes then
wipe dry and fry as above.

MUTTON IN COCONUT CURRY

750 g (1½ lb) mutton shoulder
1 teaspoon salt
3 cups thin coconut milk
4 cloves garlic, sliced
1 cm (½ inch) piece fresh ginger, shredded
6 dried chillies, soaked and mashed
½ teaspoon turmeric powder
10 cm (4 inch) stalk lemon grass, quartered
4 curry leaves
¾ teaspoon fenugreek seeds, crushed
5 cm (2 inch) stick cinnamon
1 medium onion, sliced
1 cup thick coconut milk
salt
lemon juice
1 tablespoon coconut oil or *ghee*

Trim mutton and cut into 2.5 cm (1 inch) cubes. Sprinkle with salt and place in a saucepan. Pour on thin coconut milk and add garlic, ginger and mashed chillies. Colour with turmeric powder and add half each of lemon grass, curry leaves, fenugreek seeds and cinnamon stick. Add sliced onion, reserving a little for garnish. Cover and simmer until lamb is tender, stirring occasionally.

Add thick coconut milk and season to taste with salt and lemon juice. Heat *ghee* and fry remaining lemon grass, crumbled curry leaves, fenugreek seeds, cinnamon stick and onion for 4 minutes. Stir into the curry and cook for a further 15 minutes on low heat.

MUTTON KOFTA CURRY

500 g (1 lb) boneless shoulder of mutton
1 thick slice bread
¼ cup milk
1 medium onion
5 cloves garlic
1 teaspoon chilli powder
2 teaspoons *garam masala*
1 teaspoon salt
gram flour *(besan)*, as needed
1-2 eggs
ghee for deep frying
3 large onions
2.5 cm (1 inch) piece fresh ginger
2 tablespoons *ghee*
1 tablespoon coriander, ground
2 teaspoons *garam masala*
1 teaspoon chilli powder
2 medium tomatoes
¼ cup plain yoghurt
¾ cup water
salt
pepper
sugar
½ cup thick cream
2 tablespoons finely chopped fresh coriander leaves
chilli powder

Mince or chop mutton until very smooth. Soak bread in milk then squeeze out and add to the meat with minced onion and 2 cloves garlic. Stir in chilli powder, *garam masala* and salt and bind with eggs and enough gram flour to hold the mixture together. Knead to a smooth paste and form into small balls, then flatten each slightly.

Heat *ghee* and drop in several meatballs at a time. Cook to a rich golden brown. Lift out and drain well.

Thinly slice one large onion and mince remaining onions and garlic with ginger. Heat 2 tablespoons *ghee* and fry sliced onion until soft. Add minced onion, ginger and garlic and fry for 3 minutes, stirring. Add coriander, *garam masala* and chilli powder and simmer for 3 minutes.

Peel tomatoes and chop finely. Add to pan with yoghurt and water. Bring to the boil, reduce heat and simmer for 10 minutes. Add salt, pepper and sugar to taste and stir in cream and coriander leaves. Add fried meatballs and simmer until heated through.

Garnish with chilli powder.

Mutton kofta curry (recipe this page).

BEEF AND PORK

CRISP FRIED BEEF IN TOMATO AND CHILLI SAUCE

500 g (1 lb) frying steak
1 teaspoon salt
pinch of pepper
3 tablespoons *ghee*
1 large onion, thinly sliced
2 fresh red chillies
2 cloves garlic
1 cm (½ inch) piece fresh ginger
1½ teaspoons *garam masala*
1 teaspoon cummin seeds, toasted
1 teaspoon mustard seeds, toasted
3 large tomatoes, peeled
¼ cup beef stock
salt
lemon juice

Cut beef steak into thin slices and sprinkle with salt and pepper. Heat *ghee* and fry beef slices several at a time until very dark brown and slightly crisp. Set aside, keeping warm.

Drain off most of the *ghee* and add onion. Fry until very soft. Grind chillies, garlic and ginger to a paste and add to the pan, frying for 3 minutes. Sprinkle on *garam masala*, cummin and mustard seeds and fry for 1 minute.

Chop tomato finely and add to the pan with stock and salt to taste. Simmer for 5 minutes, then return beef slices and cook for a further 15 minutes on low heat, covered tightly. Sprinkle with lemon juice to taste.

Stuffed ladies fingers, and cream curry of mushrooms, peas and tomato (recipes page 30).

SPICED PORK

ASSAD

750 g (1½ lb) pork shoulder
salt
2.5 cm (1 inch) piece fresh ginger
8 cloves garlic
1 teaspoon turmeric powder
¼ teaspoon white pepper
3 tablespoons *ghee*
5 cm (2 inch) stick cinnamon
3 cloves
6 dried chillies
2 blades mace
1½ cups water

Wipe pork and trim. Rub with a little salt. Grind ginger and garlic to a paste with turmeric and pepper and rub into the pork. Heat *ghee* and fry meat until well coloured all over.

Transfer to a deep pot and add spices and water. Cover and bring to the boil. Simmer until meat is completely tender. Lift out and drain. Slice thickly before serving.

GOAN MEAT CURRY

SORPOTEL

This is a famous dish from Goa which should be prepared several days in advance to bring out the full flavour.

750 g (1½ lb) pork, slightly fatty
250 g (½ lb) pigs liver (in one piece)
1 tablespoon coriander
1½ teaspoons cummin
1 teaspoon black peppercorns
3 tablespoons malt vinegar
1 teaspoon turmeric powder
3 green chillies
4 cloves garlic
1 cm (½ inch) piece fresh ginger
3 tablespoons *ghee*
2 teaspoons tamarind or lemon juice to taste
sugar
salt

Cut pork into reasonably large pieces and place in a saucepan with the piece of liver. Cover with water to just above the level of the meat and bring to the boil. Reduce heat and simmer for about 1½ hours until pork is tender. Remove meat, retaining the stock. Cut meat and liver into 1 cm (½ inch) dice.

Toast coriander, cummin and peppercorns under the griller for 3 minutes, then grind to a fine powder. Mix with vinegar and add turmeric. Mince chillies with garlic and ginger and fry in *ghee* for 3 minutes. Add spice powder and meat and fry until meat is well coloured.

Add the reserved stock and tamarind or lemon juice, and boil for 45 minutes, or until meat is very tender and liquid well reduced. Season to taste with sugar and salt and heat through again. Leave to cool, then cover and refrigerate for at least one day, but preferably up to three days before using.

Reheat before serving.

VEGETABLES

BRAISED PUMPKIN

625 g (1¼ lb) pumpkin
3 cloves garlic
3 dried chillies, soaked
1 medium onion
1 large onion
2 tablespoons *ghee*
1 teaspoon salt
¼ teaspoon black pepper
1 teaspoon tamarind
2 tablespoons boiling water
¾ cup water
1 tablespoon chopped fresh coriander leaves

Peel and slice pumpkin. Grind garlic, chillies and medium onion to a paste. Slice large onion thinly and fry in *ghee* until soft. Add pumpkin pieces and fry until lightly coloured, then add seasoning paste and stir on moderate heat for 2 minutes.

Season with salt, pepper and tamarind mixed with boiling water. Cover with water and bring to the boil. Simmer uncovered until pumpkin is tender, allowing most of the liquid to evaporate. Adjust seasonings, adding a little sugar if necessary.

Garnish with chopped coriander leaves.

TOMATO AND ONION SALAD

LACHUMBER

3 medium tomatoes
2 medium onions
3 green chillies
vinegar or tamarind water
salt
sugar

Peel and finely chop tomatoes and onions. Slice chillies thinly, discarding seeds. Mix vinegar or tamarind water, salt and sugar to taste and pour over the vegetables. Leave to stand for 1 hour before serving.

Serve as a side dish with any main dishes.

SPICED POTATOES
ALOO CHAT

500 g (1 lb) potatoes, peeled
2½ tablespoons *ghee*
1 large onion, minced
2 cloves garlic, minced
2 teaspoons *chat masala*
1 teaspoon turmeric powder
1 teaspoon chilli powder
1½ teaspoons salt
1 bay leaf, crumbled
½ teaspoon freshly ground black pepper
1 fresh red chilli, finely chopped
1 tablespoon finely chopped fresh coriander leaves

Cut potatoes into 2.5 cm (1 inch) cubes. Heat *ghee* and fry potato until well coloured and slightly crisp. Add onion and garlic and cook for 1 minute. Sprinkle on spices and add bay leaf. Cover pan and cook on low heat until tender. If needed, sprinkle on a little water. Shake the pan to turn potatoes. Do not open saucepan until done.

Serve with a sprinkling of black pepper and garnish with chopped chilli and coriander leaves.

MASALA POTATO WITH OKRA

2 large potatoes
250 g (½ lb) okra
3 green chillies
1 tablespoon fresh coriander leaves
1 large onion
1 large tomato
2 cloves garlic
1 cm (½ inch) piece fresh ginger
2 tablespoons *ghee*
2 teaspoons *chat masala*
½ teaspoon turmeric powder
1 cup water
sugar
salt

Peel potatoes and cut into 2.5 cm (1 inch) cubes. Wash okra and remove stems, slit lengthways. Cut green chillies into thin slices, removing seeds for milder taste. Chop coriander and slice onion and tomato. Crush garlic and shred ginger.

Heat *ghee* and fry sliced onion for 2 minutes. Add garlic and ginger and fry for a further 2 minutes, then sprinkle on *chat masala* and turmeric. Stir on high heat for 1 minute.

Add potatoes and okra and pour on water. Add chopped coriander leaves and tomato. Season to taste with sugar and salt and bring to the boil. Reduce heat and simmer until potatoes and okra are tender.

Serve with the sauce or cook until the liquid has almost evaporated.

EGGPLANT CURRY

500 g (1 lb) eggplant
1 teaspoon salt
1 teaspoon saffron powder
3 tablespoons *ghee* or oil
4 shallots, thinly sliced
3 cloves garlic, thinly sliced
2.5 cm (1 inch) piece fresh ginger, thinly sliced
8 dried chillies, toasted
2 teaspoons mustard seeds, toasted
2 teaspoons fish floss or dried shrimps, ground
10 cm (4 inch) stalk lemon grass
½ teaspoon fenugreek seeds, lightly crushed
1½ cups thin coconut milk
lemon juice
salt

Wipe eggplant and remove stems. Slice diagonally into 1 cm (½ inch) slices. Sprinkle with salt and leave for 10 minutes to draw bitter juices. Wipe off liquid and sprinkle slices with saffron powder.

Heat *ghee* or oil and fry eggplant until well coloured. Drain well. Fry shallots and garlic for 1 minute, then add ginger and chillies with all seasonings and stir on moderate heat for 1 minute. Pour in coconut milk and bring to a gentle boil. Simmer for 5 minutes. Add eggplant and cook until tender.

Season to taste with lemon juice and salt.

DRY VEGETABLE CURRY

250 g (½ lb) cauliflower
3 medium potatoes
2 medium onions
125 g (¼ lb) green beans
2.5 cm (1 inch) piece fresh ginger
2 tablespoons *ghee*
1½ teaspoons salt
2 tomatoes
¾ teaspoon turmeric
½ teaspoon chilli powder
½ teaspoon mustard seeds
2 teaspoons *garam masala*

Break cauliflower into florets and rinse in cold water. Peel and cube potato. Slice onions thickly. Cut beans into 5 cm (2 inch) pieces. Shred ginger. Heat *ghee* and fry onions and ginger for 2 minutes. Add potato and cook until lightly coloured. Add cauliflower and beans with salt and cook briefly. Peel and slice tomato and add to the pan with turmeric, chilli powder and mustard seeds. Cover and cook until the vegetables are tender but retain some crispness.

Sprinkle on *garam masala* and cook, uncovered, until the liquid has dried up completely. Stir carefully to avoid breaking the vegetables.

CREAM CURRY OF MUSHROOMS, PEAS AND TOMATO

SHABNAB

185 g (6 oz) canned champignons
185 g (6 oz) frozen green peas
6 medium tomatoes
3 tablespoons *ghee*
1 ½ teaspoons *garam masala*
¼ teaspoon fennel
pinch of salt and pepper
⅓ teaspoon turmeric powder
¾ cup thick cream
1 tablespoon finely chopped fresh coriander leaves
½ teaspoon chilli powder (optional)

Drain champignons. Thaw peas. Drop tomatoes into boiling water, count to eight and lift out. Peel and cut into wedges, discarding seeds if preferred.

Heat *ghee* and fry *garam masala* and fennel for 1 minute. Add tomato and fry until slightly softened. Add champignons and peas and cook briefly, then season with salt and pepper. Add turmeric and cream and simmer until heated through.

Stir in chopped coriander leaves and garnish with a sprinkling of chilli powder.

STUFFED LADIES FINGERS

BAHMIA

375 g (¾ lb) large okra
2 medium tomatoes
1 tablespoon brown sugar
2 tablespoons lemon juice
2 teaspoons fennel seeds, coarsely ground
¾ teaspoon turmeric powder
1 tablespoon coriander, ground
1 tablespoon *ghee*
salt
chilli powder
2 tablespoons beef stock

Wash okra, trim tops and cut a slit along each piece. Peel and finely chop tomato and mix with brown sugar, lemon juice and spices. Stuff the mixture into the okra and place in a fireproof dish.

Melt *ghee* and add to the dish. Sprinkle on salt and chilli powder and add beef stock. Cover and cook in a moderate oven or over moderate heat until the okra are tender, then remove lid and continue cooking until the pan juices are absorbed.

TOMATO PUREE

TAMATAR BURTHA

4 large tomatoes
2 large onions
1 clove garlic
1 green chilli
1 heaped teaspoon cummin, ground
1 teaspoon mustard seeds, toasted
1½ tablespoons *ghee*
1 tablespoon finely chopped fresh mint or coriander
   leaves
salt
sugar

Peel tomatoes and chop. Mince or finely chop onions, garlic and chilli. Heat oil and fry onion paste for 2 minutes, then add tomato with cummin and mustard. Simmer, stirring continually, until the mixture becomes a smooth sauce. Add a very little water if needed.

   Stir in chopped mint or coriander leaves and season to taste with salt and sugar.

VEGETABLE CUTLETS IN CURRY SAUCE

500 g (1 lb) potatoes
½ teaspoon chilli powder
2 teaspoons salt
½ teaspoon pepper
2 teaspoons *garam masala*
3 tablespoons finely chopped fresh coriander leaves
2 eggs
gram flour *(besan)*
oil or *ghee*

Curry Sauce:
1 large onion
2.5 cm (1 inch) piece fresh ginger
4 cloves garlic
2 teaspoons *garam masala*
½ teaspoon fennel
3 tablespoons *ghee*
3 tomatoes
¾ cup cream
½ teaspoon turmeric powder
chilli powder

Peel potatoes and boil until soft. Drain and mash. Add chilli powder, salt, pepper, *garam masala* and coriander and bind the mixture with egg and gram flour. Shape into cutlets.

   Heat about 2.5 cm (1 inch) oil or *ghee* in a pan, and fry cutlets until golden brown. Turn to colour evenly. Lift out and drain well.

   Prepare Curry Sauce. Mince onion with ginger and garlic. Add *garam masala* and fennel and fry in *ghee* for 4 minutes, stirring frequently. Peel tomatoes, chop finely and add to the pan. Fry for 4 minutes. Add about 4 tablespoons water and bring to the boil, then reduce heat and stir in cream. Season to taste with salt and pepper and add turmeric. Stir well. Place vegetable cutlets in the sauce and heat through.

   Transfer to a serving dish and garnish with chilli powder.

AUBERGINE PUREE
BRINJAL BURTHA

375 g (¾ lb) aubergines
2 medium onions
3 cloves garlic
2 tablespoons *ghee*
1 cm (½ inch) piece fresh ginger
2 teaspoons cummin, ground
1½ teaspoons *garam masala*
1½ teaspoons salt
2 spring onions, finely shredded
fresh coriander or mint leaves, finely chopped

Wipe eggplant and place under a moderate grill to cook until the skin is very dark and flesh completely soft. Peel off skin, discard stems and mash pulp or puree in a liquidiser.

Mince onions and garlic and fry in *ghee* for 2 minutes. Add minced ginger and eggplant puree and season with cummin. Simmer for 5 minutes on moderately low heat, then sprinkle on *garam masala* and salt. Add spring onion and cook for another 2 minutes.

Garnish with chopped coriander or mint.

GREEN VEGETABLES WITH COCONUT
MALLUNG

500 g (1 lb) mixed green vegetables
3 tablespoons vegetable or coconut oil
4 green chillies
75 g (2½ oz) freshly grated or desiccated coconut
3 teaspoons powdered dried prawns or fish floss
¾ teaspoon saffron powder
1 large onion
6 curry leaves (optional)
1 teaspoon salt
½ cup water
lemon juice
salt

Wash and coarsely shred vegetables, such as cabbage, spinach, beans, kale, etc.

Heat oil and fry slit green chillies for 5 minutes. Pour off most of the oil. Add vegetables and all ingredients except lemon juice and salt. Cover and simmer until vegetables are tender and coconut moist.

Add lemon juice and salt to taste.

SPINACH WITH COTTAGE CHEESE

SAAG PANEER

1.5 kg (3 lb) fresh spinach or
   500 g (1 lb) frozen spinach
3 tablespoons *ghee*
185 g (6 oz) prepared *paneer*
1 clove garlic
1 cm (½ inch) piece fresh ginger
1 tablespoon chopped fresh coriander leaves (optional)
½ teaspoon chilli powder
¼ teaspoon freshly grated nutmeg
½ cup thick cream
salt
pepper

Wash fresh spinach in several lots of cold water and shake out excess liquid. Shred and simmer with 1 tablespoon *ghee* and a very little water until completely tender. If using frozen spinach, place the unthawed block in a pan with 1 tablespoon *ghee,* cover and simmer until thawed. Remove lid and cook until most of the liquid has evaporated.

Cut *paneer* into 2.5 cm (1 inch) cubes. Grind garlic, ginger and coriander (if used) to a paste and add chilli and nutmeg. Heat remaining *ghee* and fry seasoning paste for 2 minutes. Add *paneer* cubes and fry until lightly coloured, then put in spinach and heat through. Stir in cream and check seasoning. Heat through before serving.

For a smoother sauce, blend spinach with cream in a liquidiser before adding to the pan to heat.

YOGHURT SALAD WITH ONION AND MINT

RAITA

2 cups plain yoghurt
3 spring onions, minced
2 tablespoons finely chopped fresh mint
½ teaspoon salt
1 teaspoon sugar
¼ teaspoon black pepper
½ teaspoon cummin, ground

Beat yoghurt until smooth then stir in all remaining ingredients. Beat for 1 minute then refrigerate. Add 2 tablespoons thick cream for a richer sauce. Serve as a side dish with any main course.

Yoghurt side dishes may include any of the following ingredients: finely chopped tomato or pineapple, grated cucumber, cooked peas with mint, cooked finely diced potato, grated apple, chopped banana, or they can simply be flavoured with spices.

BREADS

WHOLEWHEAT UNLEAVENED BREAD

CHUPATI

Makes about 12.

250 g (½ lb) wholewheat flour *(atta)*
about ¾ cup warm water
ghee

Sieve flour into a bowl and add enough water to make a soft, workable dough. Knead for at least 6 minutes until dough is very soft and will lift from the board without sticking. Cover with a damp cloth and leave for 1 hour.

Divide dough into twelve pieces and roll into balls. Roll each piece out very thinly in a circular shape with a floured rolling pin. Stack between greaseproof paper.

Heat a heavy frying pan or hot plate and cook the Chupati on each side until brown flecks appear. Transfer to a hot grill until the Chupati blow up like a balloon. Spread with a little *ghee* then wrap in a cloth until needed.

CHUPATI STUFFED WITH SEASONED POTATO

Chupati dough (see preceding recipe)

Filling:
185 g (6 oz) mashed potato
3 teaspoons coriander, ground
1 teaspoon cummin, ground
1 teaspoon salt
2 tablespoons finely choppped fresh coriander leaves
ghee

Prepare Chupati dough and break into 16 pieces. Roll each out very thinly on a floured board.

Mix potato with seasonings, adding a very little *ghee* to make a smooth paste. Spread the paste thickly over half the Chupati, leaving a narrow border. Damp this border and press another Chupati on top. Heat a heavy frying pan or hot plate and cook Chupati on both sides until dark brown flecks appear. Transfer to a hot grill to make them puff up slightly. Brush with a little *ghee* and wrap in a cloth until needed.

WHOLEWHEAT BREADS
PARATHA

Makes about 10.

250 g (½ lb) wholemeat flour *(atta)*
lukewarm water
ghee
large pinch of salt

Sieve flour into a bowl and add lukewarm water to make a slightly stiff dough. Add salt and a little *ghee* and work the dough for 4 minutes. Divide into ten pieces and roll each out to about 20 cm (8 inch) discs. Brush with a little warmed *ghee* on one side. Cover with a damp cloth and leave for at least ½ hour.

Pleat the bread at two sides to form a pleated sausage shape then twist into a circle. Roll out or press flat with buttered fingers. Bake on a hot plate or heavy frying pan over moderate heat until brown and slightly crisp underneath. Turn and cook top. Place under a hot grill to make the bread puff up slightly.

Brush with more *ghee* and wrap in a cloth until needed.

PARATHA STUFFED WITH CAULIFLOWER
GOBI WALLA PARATHA

Paratha dough (see preceding recipe)

Filling:
250 g (½ lb) cauliflower
1½ teaspoons salt
1 fresh red chilli, minced (optional)
ghee
½ teaspoon *garam masala*

Prepare Paratha dough and leave for ½ hour, covered with a damp cloth.

Break into about 18 pieces and roll out each into a disc about 2 mm (1/16 inch) thick.

Finely chop cauliflower. Fry with salt and chilli in 2 tablespoons *ghee* until soft. Sprinkle on *garam masala*. Leave to cool.

Cover half the bread discs with the stuffing and place a second disc over the top. Seal edges by pinching together, using a little water to stick. Roll out again very gently, taking care the dough does not tear. Brush with *ghee* and cook on each side on a hot plate or heavy frying pan. Transfer to a hot grill to crisp each side and make the breads puff up very slightly. Spread with more *ghee* and wrap in cloth until needed.

FRIED UNLEAVENED WHOLEWHEAT BREAD

PURI

Makes about 14.

315 g (10 oz) wholewheat flour *(atta)*
1 teaspoon salt
1 tablespoon softened *ghee*
warm water
ghee or oil for deep frying

Sieve flour into a bowl and add salt and softened *ghee*.
Work in with the fingers until the mixture is crumbly.
Add enough warm water to make a stiff dough. Knead
for 6 minutes.

Pull off pieces of dough and shape into walnut-sized
balls. Roll out on a lightly floured board with a floured
rolling pin until very thin. Stack between sheets of
greaseproof paper until ready to cook.

Heat *ghee* or oil to smoking point. The oil must be
very hot for these or they will not puff up properly.
Drop in one Puri at a time. Quickly splash the top with
the hot fat or oil and push the bread under the oil. It
should puff up like a ballon soon after going into the
pan. Cook briefly on one side, then turn and cook the
other side briefly. They must not be overcooked.

Lift out and drain well on absorbent paper. Keep
warm in a low oven until needed.

LEAVENED WHITE BREAD

NAAN

Makes 4-5.

250 g (½ lb) plain flour
1¼ teaspoons baking powder
½ teaspoon sugar
pinch of salt
⅓ - ½ cup plain yoghurt
1 tablespoon vegetable oil
1 egg

Sieve flour into a bowl and add baking powder, sugar
and salt. Mix in ⅓ cup yoghurt, vegetable oil and the
egg. Work with the fingers into a smooth, soft dough.
Add extra yoghurt if the dough still feels slightly stiff.
Knead for 5 minutes, then cover with a damp cloth and
leave in a warm place to rise for 4 hours.

Heat a hotplate or heavy-based frying pan. Divide
the dough into 4-5 pieces and with wet fingers pull into
an elongated triangular shape. Wet one side and stick
this down on the pan. Cook on moderate heat for about
1½ minutes, then turn pan over so the top of the bread
is exposed directly to the heat. Cook until dark brown
flecks appear and the bread is springy to the touch.

Keep in a cloth or covered box until needed.

Indian breads (recipes pages 34–37).

LEAVENED YOGHURT YEAST BREAD

KULCHA

Yoghurt Yeast:
60 g (2 oz) plain flour
1½ tablespoons warm plain yoghurt
1½ teaspoons white sugar
4 black peppercorns (optional)
1½ tablespoons warm water

Mix ingredients together, beating well. Leave in a warm place overnight. Discard peppercorns.

Yeast Bread:
250 g (½ lb) plain flour
2¼ tablespoons yoghurt yeast (see above)
1 tablespoon sugar
1 teaspoon salt
2¼ tablespoons *ghee*
¼ - ⅓ cup warm milk
ghee or oil for deep frying

Sieve flour into a bowl and add remaining ingredients. Work to a soft dough, adding more milk if needed. Knead vigorously for 7 minutes, then cover with damp cloth and leave in a warm place for 2½ hours.

Wet hands and knead again for 3 minutes. Roll out into 15 cm (6 inch) discs and leave, covered with a damp cloth, to rise again for about ½ hour.

Heat *ghee* or oil and fry Kulcha one at a time until golden and cooked through. Drain well and wrap in a cloth until needed. This makes about 6 Kulcha.

*Shrimp rice, dhal special, and spiced chickpeas
(recipes pages 41, 44 and 45).*

RICE DISHES

MUTTON BIRIYANI

375 g (¾ lb) lean mutton
¼ cup plain yoghurt
2 teaspoons lemon juice
4 teaspoons *garam masala*
1 teaspoon turmeric powder
4 cloves garlic
1 large onion
2.5 cm (1 inch) piece fresh ginger
3 tablespoons *ghee*
375 g (¾ lb) long grain rice
2 medium onions, thinly sliced
5 cm (2 inch) cinnamon stick, broken
4 cloves
2 blades mace
3 bay leaves
½ teaspoon chilli powder
3 hardboiled eggs
1 tablespoon blanched almonds, fried in *ghee*

Trim mutton and cut into 3 cm (1¼ inch) cubes. Place
in a bowl and pour on yoghurt and lemon juice.
Sprinkle on 2 teaspoons *garam masala* and the turmeric. Finely mince garlic, onion and ginger and add to
the meat. Stir well and leave to marinate for 1 hour.

Put marinated mixture into a pan, cover with water
and boil for 1½ hours. Drain, reserving stock.

Heat *ghee* and fry rice until each grain is well oiled.
Add onion, cinnamon, cloves, mace and bay leaves. Fry
for 3 minutes then add drained meat and fry until well
coloured. Pour in mutton stock and add water, if
needed, to make up 3¼ cups. Add chilli powder and
bring to the boil. Cover and reduce heat to lowest
point. Leave to cook until rice is tender and liquid completely absorbed.

Sprinkle on *garam masala* and stir meat into the rice.
Cut hardboiled eggs into wedges and decorate the rice
with egg and almonds. Serve hot.

PRAWN BIRIYANI

BIRIYANI JHINGA

750 g (1½ lb) raw prawns in shells
4½ cups water
1 large onion
6 cloves garlic
2.5 cm (1 inch) piece fresh ginger
4 dried chillies, soaked
1 teaspoon cummin
1 teaspoon black peppercorns
5 cm (2 inch) stick cinnamon
6 cloves
3 black cardamoms, crushed
¼ teaspoon saffron powder
1 tablespoon boiling water
3 tablespoons *ghee*
375 g (¾ lb) long grain rice
4 large tomatoes
salt
rose water (optional)

Remove heads and shells from prawns, leaving tails on.
Place shells and heads in a pot with water. Cover pot,
bring to the boil and then reduce heat and simmer for 1
hour. Strain, reserving liquid.

Pound onion, garlic, ginger and chillies to a paste.
Grind cummin and black peppercorns coarsely. Mix in
broken cinnamon stick, cloves and cardamoms. Mix
saffron with boiling water.

Melt *ghee* in a large pan and fry rice until grains are
well coated with the *ghee*. Add onion paste and mix
well, fry for 3 minutes, stirring constantly, then add
spice mixture and stir thoroughly. Add reserved stock
which should measure 3¼ cups. Bring to the boil and
cook until rice is almost tender and liquid absorbed.
Add prawns, sliced tomato and salt to taste and continue to cook, tightly covered, until rice is tender and
grains dry and well separated. Prawns should be pink
and cooked through.

Splash on rose water and stir before serving.

MUTTON STOCK PILLAU WITH SHRIMP AND PEAS

750 g (1½ lb) mutton bones
5 cups water
1 medium onion
4 cloves
2 cloves garlic
2 bay leaves
5 cm (2 inch) stick cinnamon
375 g (¾ lb) long grain rice
3 tablespoons *ghee*
1 large onion, thinly sliced
3 cloves garlic, thinly sliced
4 black cardamoms, crushed
2 medium tomatoes, sliced
salt
pepper
185 g (6 oz) raw shrimp, peeled
185 g (6 oz) frozen peas
30 g (1 oz) blanched, slivered almonds
30 g (1 oz) raisins, soaked
1 teaspoon rose water (optional)

Chop up mutton bones and boil for 1 hour with water, onion stuck with cloves, garlic, bay leaves and cinnamon stick. Strain stock and reduce or add water to make up to 3 ¼ cups.

Wash rice in cold water and drain well. Heat *ghee* in a heavy saucepan and fry thinly sliced onion and garlic until soft. Add rice and stir until all grains are well coated with *ghee*. Add cardamoms, tomato, salt, pepper and the 3 ¼ cups stock. Cover and bring to the boil, then reduce heat and cook until the water is absorbed and the rice is beginning to soften. Stir in shrimps and peas. Cover and continue to cook until rice is tender and shrimp and peas cooked. Stir in nuts and drained raisins and place in a hot oven for 10 minutes.

Splash on rose water and stir the dish thoroughly before serving.

YELLOW RICE

345 g (11 oz) long grain rice
¾ teaspoon saffron strands
1 tablespoon boiling water
5 cm (2 inch) stick cinnamon
4 cloves
3 black cardamoms
3 cups water
2 tablespoons *ghee*
30 g (1 oz) raisins
30 g (1 oz) blanched almonds

Soak rice in cold water for ½ hour. Drain well. Steep saffron in boiling water and grind to release the colour. Pour rice into a saucepan and add saffron water, cinnamon, cloves and cardamoms. Pour on water and bring to the boil. Cover, reduce heat and simmer until rice is tender and liquid absorbed. Transfer to a hot oven for 10 minutes.

Fry raisins and blanched almonds gently in *ghee* for 2 minutes. Stir into the rice and serve at once.

SHRIMP RICE

375 g (¾ lb) long grain rice
1 large onion
4 tablespoons *ghee*
2 cloves garlic
2.5 cm (1 inch) piece fresh ginger
250 g (½ lb) raw shrimps, peeled
½ teaspoon ground black pepper
3 cloves
5 cm (2 inch) cinnamon stick
2 green cardamoms, crushed
1 teaspoon salt
¼ cup thick coconut milk or thick cream
1 bay leaf
fresh mint or coriander leaves
red or green chilli, sliced

Wash rice and soak in cold water for 40 minutes. Drain well. Slice onion thinly and fry in *ghee* until soft. Add minced garlic and ginger and fry for 1 minute, then put in shrimps and cook until pink. Add rice and stir on moderate heat until all grains are well coated with the *ghee*. Add pepper, cloves, cinnamon, cardamoms, salt and coconut milk or thick cream. Pour on water to reach 3 cm (1¼ inches) above the level of the rice. Add bay leaf. Cover and bring to the boil, then reduce heat and cook until rice is tender and liquid absorbed.

Stir rice well, cover and place in warm oven for 15 minutes. Garnish with mint or coriander leaves and sliced chilli.

CHICKEN PILLAU

375 g (¾ lb) long grain rice
750 g (1½ lb) chicken
2 medium onions
3 cloves garlic, minced
6 tablespoons *ghee*
4 cm (1½ inch) piece fresh ginger, minced
½ cup plain yoghurt
2 teaspoons salt
½ teaspoon ground black pepper
2 bay leaves
5 cm (2 inch) stick cinnamon
4 black cardamoms, crushed
pinch of freshly grated nutmeg
2 fresh red chillies
4 shallots

Wash rice in cold water and drain well. Cut chicken into 2.5 cm (1 inch) cubes. Slice one onion and mince the other. Heat 5 tablespoons *ghee* and fry sliced onion until soft. Add minced onion and garlic and fry for 2 minutes, then put in chicken pieces and cook until well coloured.

Add ginger and yoghurt, stirring well. Pour rice into the pan and add salt, pepper, bay leaves, cinnamon, cardamoms and nutmeg. Cover to 3 cm (1¼ inches) above the level of the rice with water or light chicken stock. Cover and bring to the boil. Reduce heat and simmer until the rice is tender and chicken cooked through.

Fry sliced chillies and shallots in 1 tablespoon *ghee* or oil for 2 minutes and stir into rice.

ACCOMPANIMENTS

LEMONS PICKLED IN SALT

500 g (1 lb) small lemons
5 cm (2 inch) piece fresh ginger
6 green chillies
2 tablespoons chilli powder
500 g (1 lb) coarse salt

Wash and dry lemons and cut into quarters. Grind ginger and chillies to a paste and mix with chilli powder and salt. Place lemons in a large jar, add the seasonings and cover tightly. Shake jar to distribute seasonings and leave in a sunny place for 2-3 weeks, undisturbed, or place in a very low oven for 2 days, then store in a warm cupboard.
    Leave for about 2 months before using.

FRESH MINT CHUTNEY

90 g (3 oz) fresh mint
1 small onion
1-2 green chillies, seeds removed
2 teaspoons sugar
salt
lemon juice

Wash mint and pick off leaves, discarding stems. Chop leaves finely. Mince onion and chillies and mix with mint, adding sugar and salt and lemon juice to taste. Pound all together to a smooth paste or puree in the liquidiser.
    Serve with Samoosa or Pakora.

SPICED LENTIL SAUCE

185 g (6 oz) whole black lentils
2 cups water
1 teaspoon salt
¾ teaspoon turmeric powder
1 green chilli, sliced
2 tablespoons *ghee*
1 large onion, finely chopped
2 cloves garlic, crushed
2 teaspoons *garam masala*
pinch of chilli powder
2 tablespoons finely chopped fresh coriander leaves

Soak lentils overnight in cold water. Drain and place in a saucepan with water, salt, turmeric and chilli. Bring to the boil, then reduce heat and simmer until lentils are tender. Add a little more water if needed. Heat *ghee* and fry onion and garlic until soft. Add *garam masala* and chilli powder and fry briefly.
    Stir into the lentils and add fresh coriander leaves. Reheat before serving.

COCONUT CHUTNEY

125 g (¼ lb) grated fresh coconut, or
   90 g (3 oz) moistened desiccated coconut
1 tablespoon white poppy seeds, ground
1 heaped tablespoon finely chopped fresh coriander
   mint or leaves
¾ teaspoon mustard seeds
pinch of chilli
pinch of saffron powder
1 teaspoon cummin, ground
salt
sugar
lemon juice

Pound coconut with poppy seeds and coriander or mint leaves to a coarse paste. Add mustard seeds, chilli and saffron and cummin and mix well. Season to taste with salt and pepper and add lemon juice to moisten.

   Store in an airtight container in the refrigerator for up to 5 days.

MANGO PICKLE

AAM KA ACHAR

2 kg (4 lb) small unripe mangoes
2 tablespoons fenugreek seeds
3 teaspoons turmeric powder
½ teaspoon asafoetida
12 dried red chillies, soaked
500 g (1 lb) coarse salt
2 cups mustard oil

Cut mangoes in halves, lengthways, cutting through the stone which will still be soft if mangoes are sufficiently unripe. Mix spices with salt and about 4 tablespoons oil and cover one half of each mango with a thick layer of the paste. Press the other half on top. Arrange all stuffed mangoes in a wide-necked jar and sprinkle on any remaining spices. Cover jar and leave for 1 day.

   Heat remaining mustard oil to lukewarm and pour onto the mangoes. Seal jars again and leave in a warm sunny place for 10 days, or place in a very low oven for 2 days, then keep in a warm cupboard for 1 month.

   Store in a cool dry cupboard when ready.

CORIANDER CHUTNEY

125 g (¼ lb) fresh coriander leaves
1 teaspoon salt
3 cloves garlic
1 cm (½ inch) piece fresh ginger
1-2 teaspoons sugar
lemon or lime juice

Wash coriander leaves and shake out water. Chop finely, then pound to a paste with remaining ingredients, adding lemon juice to taste. This can be prepared in the blender.

   Keep refrigerated in an airtight container for up to 3 days.

DHAL AND CHICKPEAS

DHAL SPECIAL

250 g (½ lb) red or yellow lentils
2 medium onions
2 cloves garlic
1 green chilli
3 tablespoons *ghee*
1 tablespoon coriander, ground
1 teaspoon turmeric powder
1 teaspoon cummin, ground
salt
pepper
¼ cup thick cream
2 teaspoons coriander seeds
4 shallots, thinly sliced
1 tablespoon *ghee*

Wash lentils and cover with water to about 4 cm (1½ inches) above the level of the lentils. Bring to the boil and cook until very soft, then drain well, reserving the liquid.

Mince onions, garlic and chilli and fry in *ghee* for 3 minutes. Add spices and fry for 2 minutes, then pour in lentil mixture and heat through. Mash to a smooth puree and season to taste with salt and pepper. Stir in cream and some of the reserved liquid if too thick. The Dhal should have the consistency of a thick soup.

Fry coriander seeds and sliced shallots in *ghee* for 1 minute and stir into the Dhal.

DHAL CURRY WITH COCONUT

220 g (7 oz) red lentils
1¾ cups thin coconut milk
1 tablespoon dried shrimp, soaked and coarsely ground
½ teaspoon saffron powder
1 green chilli, thinly sliced
2.5 cm (1 inch) stalk lemon grass, finely chopped
1 cup thick coconut milk
salt
black pepper
2 curry leaves
4 shallots, sliced
chilli powder
1 tablespoon *ghee*

Wash lentils well and soak in cold water to cover for 2 hours. Drain well and put into a saucepan with thin coconut milk, dried shrimp, saffron, chilli and lemon grass. Bring to the boil, then cover and leave to simmer until lentils are almost tender. Add thick coconut milk, salt and pepper and continue to cook until done.

Crumble bay leaves and fry in *ghee* with sliced shallots for 2 minutes. Stir into the Dhal and add chilli powder to taste. Heat through briefly.

SPICED CHICKPEAS

KABLI CHANNA

625 g (1¼ lb) canned chickpeas
1 large onion
5 cm (2 inch) piece fresh ginger
2 cloves garlic
3 tablespoons *ghee*
1 teaspoon pomegranate seeds, ground, or
   1 tablespoon lemon juice
1½ teaspoons *garam masala*
¾ teaspoon dried green mango powder *(amchur)*
2 green chillies, sliced
2 large tomatoes, peeled
3 tablespoons chopped fresh coriander leaves
salt
black pepper
chilli powder (optional)

Drain chickpeas, reserving a little of the liquid. Slice onion thinly. Shred or grate ginger and crush garlic. Fry onion, ginger and garlic in *ghee* until soft then add pomegranate seeds (if using lemon juice do not add at this point), *garam masala* and mango powder. Stir on moderate heat for 1 minute then put in drained chick-peas. Stir until well coated with the spices. Add sliced chillies and pour in the reserved chickpea liquid and enough water to just cover. Bring to the boil, reduce heat, and simmer for 10 minutes.

Chop tomatoes coarsely and add to the pan with coriander leaves, salt, pepper and lemon juice (if used). Continue to cook for a further 15 minutes.

Garnish with chilli powder. Leave overnight if time allows, and reheat before serving, for extra flavour.

DESSERTS

CARROT DESSERT

GAJAR HALWA

750 g (1½ lb) carrots
8 cups milk
3 tablespoons full cream milk powder
5 cm (2 inch) stick cinnamon
125 g (¼ lb) raisins, soaked
3 black cardamoms, crushed lightly
½ teaspoon saffron powder
1 tablespoon boiling water
3 tablespoons *ghee* or butter
2 tablespoons honey
185 g (6 oz) sugar, or to taste
90 g (3 oz) blanched, slivered almonds
1½ teaspoons rose water
silver leaf to decorate (optional)

Scrape carrots, rinse, then grate finely. Put into a saucepan and pour on milk. Add milk powder and cinnamon stick. Bring to the boil and cook, stirring frequently, until the mixture has thickened and carrot is beginning to become very soft. Add drained raisins, cardamoms and saffron mixed with boiling water and continue to cook, stirring continually, until the mixture becomes a thick paste.

Add *ghee*, honey and sugar and cook again, stirring, until thick. Stir in blanched almonds and rose water. Spoon into a lightly buttered dish and smooth the top. Decorate with silver leaf if available. Leave to cool before serving, or serve hot.

FRIED SWEET BATTER CURLS

JALEBI

250 g (½ lb) plain flour
2 teaspoons baking powder
1 heaped teaspoon saffron powder
2 tablespoons warm water
oil or *ghee* for deep frying
185 g (6 oz) sugar
1½ cups water
1 teaspoon rose water

Sieve flour and baking powder into a basin. Infuse saffron in warm water and pour over the flour. Add enough water to make a smooth batter which is thick enough to squeeze through a forcing pipe. Leave for 30 minutes.

Heat oil or *ghee* and fill forcing bag with the batter. Pipe swirls of batter into the oil and lift out after about 1½ minutes. They should be crisp and well puffed out. Drain on absorbent paper.

Pour sugar and water into a saucepan and bring to the boil. Simmer for 5 minutes, then remove from heat and splash in rose water. Leave to cool. Arrange Jalebi in a serving dish and pour on the syrup. Chill slightly before serving.

COCONUT TOFFEE

NARIAL KI BARFI

125 g (¼ lb) desiccated coconut
155 g (5 oz) sugar
½ - ¾ cup water
1 green cardamom, ground
pink food colouring

Moisten coconut slightly with water. Pour sugar and water into a small saucepan and cook on low heat without stirring until the syrup is sticky. To test if ready dab a little onto the back of a wooden spoon. Press a finger onto it and draw away. When thin threads of toffee are formed between spoon and finger, syrup is the correct consistency. Add moistened coconut and stir until mixture is thick. Stir in cardamom.

Spread half onto a greased tray and colour the other half pink. Pour on top and press flat. Mark out squares before completely set and cut when cold.

HALVA WITH PISTACHIOS

375 g (¾ lb) sugar
1¼ cups water
315 g (10 oz) full cream milk powder
5 tablespoons *ghee*
¾ teaspoon powdered cardamom
45 g (1½ oz) pistachios

Pour sugar and water into a saucepan and bring to the boil. Cook until lightly coloured and beginning to thicken. Beat in milk powder and *ghee* and continue beating over moderate heat until the mixture is smooth. Lower heat very slightly and stir until the mixture resembles a thick, light brown fudge and leaves the sides of the pan.

Finely chop or crush two-thirds of the pistachios and stir into the Halva. Heat through, then spoon into a greased tray 23 cm (9 inches) square, and spread out smoothly. Decorate the top with remaining pistachios and leave to cool. When set cut into squares.

BUTTERY PEA FLOUR FUDGE

MYSORE PAK

440 g (14 oz) *ghee*
125 g (¼ lb) gram flour *(besan)*
315 g (10 oz) sugar
¾ cup water

Melt one-third of the *ghee* and fry flour until lightly coloured. Melt remaining *ghee* and set aside.

Pour sugar and water into a saucepan and bring to the boil. Cook without stirring until very sticky and beginning to darken. Test if right by dabbing a little on the back of a wooden spoon. Press a finger on and pull away. The toffee should form into long firm threads between finger and spoon.

Add fried flour and melted *ghee* and cook on moderate heat, stirring continually, until very thick.

Pour into a buttered square tray and press flat. Cut into squares when set and serve when completely cold.

MILK BALLS IN SUGAR SYRUP
GULAB JAMON

185 g (6 oz) full cream milk powder
2 tablespoons *ghee*
125 g (¼ lb) self-raising flour
1 teaspoon baking powder
vegetable oil for deep frying
315 g (10 oz) sugar
1¾ cups water
1½ teaspoons rose water

Mix milk powder with *ghee* and work to a crumbly texture. Add self-raising flour and baking powder and mix well, crumbling with the fingers. Mix in a very little water to make a very stiff dough. Wrap in a damp cloth and leave for 3 hours.

Break the dough and rub hard on a floured board into fine crumbs. Add sprinkling of water and form mixture into walnut-sized balls. Heat oil and deep fry balls to a light golden brown. Shake pan during cooking to colour the balls evenly. Lift out and drain well.

Pour sugar and water into a saucepan and bring to the boil. Simmer until very slightly sticky. Splash in rose water and add milk balls. Leave milk balls to soak in the syrup for at least ½ hour before serving. Serve warm or chilled.

CREAM BALLS IN CREAM SAUCE
RAS MALAI

125 g (¼ lb) full cream milk powder
30 g (1 oz) self-raising flour
⅓ cup whole milk
250 g (½ lb) white sugar
1¼ cups water
3 cups milk
½ cup thick cream
1½ teaspoons rose water
1 tablespoon blanched, chopped almonds

Mix milk powder and self-raising flour with up to ⅓ cup milk, adding milk gradually to make a dough which just holds together. Wrap in a damp cloth and leave for 3 hours.

Break the dough and crumble with the fingers, then with wet hands form into walnut-sized balls.

Pour sugar and water into a saucepan and bring to the boil. Add cream balls and simmer for 15 minutes, shaking pan to turn the balls. Splash in about 1 tablespoon ice water, which should make the balls puff out a little. Lift out and leave to cool.

Bring milk to the boil and add enough of the sugar syrup to sweeten to taste. Return cream balls and leave in this liquid for another 3 hours.

Remove the cream balls again and boil milk until well reduced. Stir in cream and add rose water and chopped nuts. Return balls and allow to cool before serving. This is best served slightly chilled.

*Carrot dessert, and cream balls in cream sauce
(recipes page 46 and this page).*

CREAM BALLS IN SUGAR SYRUP

RAS GULLA

cream balls from Ras Malai
375 g (¾ lb) white sugar
2 cups water
1 teaspoon cornflour
1 teaspoon rose water

Prepare the cream ball dough and shape into balls as directed. Pour sugar and water into a saucepan and bring to the boil. Simmer for 5 minutes, then put in the cream balls. Simmer for 15 minutes until the balls rise to the surface and are slightly expanded. Mix cornflour with a little cold water and stir into the syrup to thicken very slightly.

Remove from the heat and stir in rose water. Chill before serving. Serve the cream balls with a little of the syrup.

RICE PUDDING

KHEER

90 g (3 oz) short grain rice
3¼ cups fresh whole milk
2 green cardamoms
75 g (2½ oz) sugar

Wash rice and soak for ½ hour in cold water. Bring milk to a rolling boil and pour in drained rice and cardamoms. Cover and simmer until rice is completely soft.

Stir in sugar and continue cooking for 5 more minutes. Serve hot or cold.

STEAMED YOGHURT SWEET

BARPHI DAHI

4 cups fresh whole milk
125 g (¼ lb) sugar
1 cup plain yoghurt
12 blanched, slivered almonds
15 g (½ oz) raisins
1 tablespoon *ghee*

Bring milk to boil and continue to cook until reduced by half. Stir in sugar and cook until dissolved. Beat yoghurt and add to the milk mixture. Pour into a buttered fireproof dish and cover with foil. Place in a dish of water in a moderately hot oven and cook until the pudding sets.

Fry almonds and raisins in *ghee* and sprinkle over the pudding. Cook for a further 5 minutes. Serve hot or well chilled.

A selection of ingredients for curries.

GLOSSARY

AMCHUR: Powdered seasoning made from dried green mangoes. It has a sharp, slightly tangy taste, and is used as condiment on roasted foods and frequently in pickles.

ASAFOETIDA: Gum-like substance. Can be omitted.

ATTA: Fine wholewheat flour.

BESAN: A fine yellow flour made from chickpeas or gabanzos.

CARDAMOM: An aromatic spice of the Ginger family.

CHANNA: Also known as chickpeas or garbanzos. A fine yellow flour, *besan*, is made from the ground peas and used in many sweet and savoury dishes.

CHAT MASALA: A combination of spices, including ground mango powder or *amchur* and ground pomegranate seeds, with a sharp, almost astringent taste. Used with fruit and vegetables as a condiment and seasoning.

CHILLIES: Sometimes known as hot peppers, chillies can be used fresh, flaked or powdered. Fresh chillies are green (unripe) or red (ripe). The seeds, which are the hottest part, can be removed before use.

COCONUT MILK: The thick and creamy liquid made from the ground flesh of ripe coconuts mixed with water. Not to be confused with coconut water, which is the almost clear liquid found inside the nut.

CUMMIN, WHITE: Actually light brown in colour, it is a seed resembling caraway but with a different flavour. It is an important ingredient in *garam masala*.

CURRY LEAVES: A fragrant dried leaf indispensible to a good curry. Bay leaves can occasionally be suggested as a substitute, but the flavour is quite different.

CURRY PASTE: Prepared curry paste containing a mixture of spices in an oil or coconut-milk base.

FENUGREEK: Dried fenugreek seeds smell of burnt sugar and have a slightly bitter taste. The fresh leaves are interchangeable with spinach though slightly more bitter.

FISH FLOSS: Shredded dried salt fish, or fish cooked to dryness in coconut milk and then finely shredded.

GARAM MASALA: A blend of spices prepared as a curry powder or condiment. Unlike commercial curry powders, the mixture contains neither powdered turmeric nor chilli powder.

GHEE: Clarified butter. It is high in cholesterol, and vegetable oils can be substituted.

GINGER: Fresh root ginger is essential in Indian cooking, and dried powdered ginger is *not* a substitute. Fresh ginger should be peeled or scraped to remove the thin flaky skin, and the flesh sliced, finely shredded or grated.

LEMON GRASS: Also known as citronella grass. The white bulbous part is used for its lemony fragrance. It is sold dried in strip form, chopped, or powdered. Substitute lemon peel.

POPPY SEEDS, WHITE: Used as a flavouring and thickening ingredient in Indian cooking.

ROSEWATER: Fragrant, delicate essence of roses used as a flavouring for Indian sweets and occasionally in rich savoury dishes and *biriyani*.

SAFFRON: Imparts a delicate flavour and a bright orange-yellow colour. Turmeric is often substituted as a colouring agent, but do not use turmeric in sweet dishes.

TAMARIND: Semi-dried flesh from the seed pods of the tamarind tree. Mix with hot water to make a strongly flavoured acidulating liquid for tenderising meats and for adding a sourish tang to many dishes. Substitute vinegar, lime or lemon juice mixed with a little water.

TURMERIC: A bright-yellow spice with a musky fragrance and a distinctive taste, used for colouring and flavouring many curried dishes and some rice dishes. Powdered turmeric is stronger than fresh: substitute one-third to one-half powder to fresh.

YOGHURT: Plain unflavoured yoghurt is used extensively in Indian cooking as a tenderiser, enricher, thickener and sweets ingredient.

INDEX

aam ka achar 43
aloo chat 28
assad 26
aubergine puree 32

bahmia 30
barphi dahi 49
batter curls, fried sweet 46
beef, crisp fried in tomato and chilli
    sauce 25
bhindi gosht 22
biriyani jhinga 39
breads
    chupati 34
    paratha 35
    white leavened 56
    wholewheat 35
    wholewheat unleavened 34
    wholewheat unleavened, fried 34
    yoghurt yeast, leavened 37
brinjal burtha 32

carrot dessert 46
chat masala 4
chicken
    coconut curried 14
    curry 15
    Kashmir 12
    pillau 41
    tandoori 13
    tikka 15
    in white curry 14
    yoghurt 13
chickpeas, spiced 45
chupati, stuffed with seasoned
    potato 34
chutney
    coconut 43
    coriander 43
    mint, fresh 42
coconut toffee 47
crab korma 11
cream
    balls in cream sauce 48
    balls in sugar syrup 49
curry
    cream, with mushrooms, peas and
      tomato 30
    dry vegetable 29
    egg 16
    eggplant 29
    Goan fish 9
    Goan meat 26
    lamb and potato 20
    mutton in coconut 23
    mutton kofta 24
    prawn and green mango 10
    sauce, vegetable cutlets in 31

dhal curry with coconut 37
dum murghi Kashmir 12

eggplant curry 29
eggs
    masala 16
    scrambled, Parsi style 6

fish
    baked, with creamed tomato
      sauce 8
    in coconut sauce 10
    Goan curried 9
    kebabs 9
    masala stuffed 11
fudge, pea flour, buttery 47

gajar halwa 46
garam masala 4
gobi walla paratha 35
gulab jamon 48

halva with pistachios 47

jaleki 46

kabli channa 45
keema muttar 21
kheer 49
kulcha 37

lachumber 27
ladies fingers, stuffed 30; see also okra
lamb
    braised, with fruit and nuts 18
    dhansak with brown rice 19
    kebabs, minced 20
    and potato curry 20
    in spinach puree 17
lentil cakes in yoghurt sauce, cold 7

mallung 32
meat
    curry, Goan 26
    samoosa 6
    savoury minced 22
    snacks, fried 6
milk balls in sugar syrup 48
murgh mussalam 14
mushrooms in cream curry with peas
    and tomato 30
mutton
    biriyani 38
    in coconut curry 23
    with fried okra 22
    kofta curry 24
    minced, with peas 21
    stock pillau with shrimp and peas 40
Mysore pak 47

naan 36
narial ki barfi 47

okra
    fried, with mutton 22
    ladies fingers, stuffed 30
    with masala potato 28
onions
    and tomato salad 32
    with yoghurt salad and mint 33

pakora
paratha 35
    stuffed with cauliflower 35
pickles
    lemon, in salt 42
    mango 43
pork, spiced 26
potatoes
    masala, with okra 28
    spiced 28
prawns
    biriyani 38
    and green mango curry 10
    in green masala 8
pumpkin, braised 27
puri 36

raita 33
ras gulla 49
ras malai 48

rice
   biriyani, mutton 38
   biriyani, prawn 38
   pillau, chicken 41
   pillau, mutton stock with shrimp and
      peas 40
   pudding 49
   shrimp 41
   yellow 40

saag paneer 33
salads
   tomato and onion 27
   yoghurt, with onion and mint 33
samoosa 5
sorpotel 26
soup, mulligatawny 7
spinach, with cottage cheese 33

tamatar burtha 31
tomato
   and onion salad 32
   puree 31

vegetables
   curry, dry 29
   cutlets in curry sauce 31
   dumplings, fried 5
   green, with coconut 32
   snacks, crisp 5

yoghurt, steamed, sweet 49